# CHRISTIAN AND LEADERSHIP
# HIDDEN TRAPS
## *to* AVOID

## WARNING! PASTORS, CHRISTIANS AND LEADERS

# DR. TAI OLAMIGOKE

WESTBOW
PRESS®
A DIVISION OF THOMAS NELSON
& ZONDERVAN

WestBow Press books may be ordered through booksellers or by contacting:

WestBow Press
A Division of Thomas Nelson & Zondervan
1663 Liberty Drive
Bloomington, IN 47403
www.westbowpress.com
844-714-3454

All scripture quotations are taken from the King James Version.

ISBN: 978-1-9736-9876-0 (sc)
ISBN: 978-1-9736-9877-7 (e)

Library of Congress Control Number: 2023909578

Print information available on the last page.

WestBow Press rev. date: 06/07/2023

# CONTENTS

# ACKNOWLEDGEMENT

I acknowledge the spiritual and moral support of my darling wife Pastor Caroline Olamigoke who is always in full support of my dedicated work to God.

**To all members, ministers, elders of House of David, I acknow- ledge your love and support. God mightily bless you in Jesus name.**

To my Siblings both in the USA and Africa thank you for your prayers and support.

To all the men and women of God who were with us during persecution: Pastors (Dr) and (Mrs.) E.A. Adeboye, Pastor (Dr) James Fadele, Pastor Okonrende, Pastor & Pastor Mrs. K Sanusi, Pastor Bayo Fadugba, Pastor Dave Arogbonlo, Pastor (Dr.) Christy Ogbeide, Pastor Soyebo, Pastor Remi Adesola, Pastor Gbenga Kuye, Pastor Benson Akintunji, Pastor Tope Adegbamigbe that called, prayed and encouraged us.

To my two children that make parenting easy and interesting, you are the best. To God be all the glory forever and ever.

# PREFACE

God gave me this title: Pastoral/Leadership/Christian Hidden Traps in the Ministry during the time of persecution in the ministry. This book must be read by any leader either at home, work, but especially in the Ministry. You must read this book before you say **"I do" and plunge into the ministry.**

Christian leaders, business leaders or Head of families (Husband), should be conscious of the fact that the plan of the enemy is to bring people down. He is into the business of destroying lives, homes and ministries.

Satan is an expert in setting traps. He set them in order to catch ministers whose desire is to serve God. Since he knows that men and women of God will do everything possible to avoid his traps, he therefore uses the hidden traps to lure them to do his will. God wants our standard to be higher than the world.

The Bible I read at the age of six has not changed, so why should we live a different life today. Why are men and women of God, including Christians, Parents, and Principals, lowering the high standard set by God?

We must note that this book is not only for Pastors and leaders in the Church, but also for every believer whom God calls the head and not the tail. Most Christians are leaders in the secular world and at home; however the principle of God should be applied in all area whether at home or the church.

The work of the ministry has become more challeng-ing today. Many go into it with a clean heart and a willingness to serve and obey God only to find out that they are off track.

An article was sent to me by a Pastor recently about reasons why Pastors quit too soon. Over 1,700 Pastors leave the ministry every month according to statistics. I believe this is in the USA; although 4000 new churches begin each year. We will address some of the reasons they quit in the following pages. Some of the reasons they quit are as follows:

- Discouragement
- Failure
- Loneliness
- Moral Failure
- Financial Pressure
- Anger
- Burnout
- Physical Health
- Marriage/Family Problems
- Too Busy/Driven

Please relax and enjoy this Holy Spirit inspired book.

The purpose of ministry is to express elements of God's character through human hands and lips.

# CHAPTER ONE

## The Hidden Trap of Pride

The fact is that most Pastors did not start their ministries for self serving or egotistical reasons. In fact almost all the Pastors began their ministries with humility. They started from a shelter, a living room, school class room, or even in a hotel room with two, five, or more families. They had no musical equip-ment, except the natural gift from God – the hand clap. Before you know it, as you continue to abide in God, you are wining souls, caring for the people, and sharing the love of God with everyone; and people are applauding you, something then stirs up in you with a feeling of importance. Pride becomes a factor.

Pastors and ministry leaders are peculiar. They are willing to sacrifice everything, careers, possessions, family, friends, and a normal life, all to pursue the calling that God has placed in their hearts. This calling, this passion, flows through their veins with every beat of their hearts, increasing their longing to reach the goal.

When hard times come, they press on instead of giving up. When good times are upon them, they give all of the honor and glory to God Almighty rather than themselves.

Their lives are full of faith and perseverance. However, as time passes and the attention shifts from excitement for the vision to more mundane things, many leaders begin to change their character, forgetting past perspectives and trading them for "more seasoned" ideas about ministry life. These ideas are sometimes borrowed from other leaders. Sometimes, they come as a result of the hardships that ministers have endured to keep their vision alive. Other times, these ways of thought are misperceptions and a lack of alertness, causing them to fall into errant ways that form the perfect breeding ground for pride, envy, and deceit.

Love of praise is equally very deadly: and more so because it is part of daily life. But we should not underestimate the addictive power of applause. John Chrysostom wrote, "I do not know whether anyone has ever succeeded in not enjoying Praise. And if he enjoys it, he naturally wants to receive it. And if he wants to receive it, he cannot help being pained and distraught at losing it…Men who are in love with applause have their spirits starved not only when they are blamed off-hand, but even when they fail to be constantly praised."

Understanding, the threat to the ministry a sensible man of God looks up to Christ for defense. Christ was tempted in all things, including vainglory, and He prevailed every time (**Hebrew 4:15).** Accordingly, ministers who feel the weight of their charge or calling will incline their ears every time to their Lord who tells them to **"Beware."** He does so in **Matthew 6:1,** when He warns us to "beware of practicing our righteousness before men, to be noticed by them." Here Jesus has identified a virtual minefield for the Pastor, whose time is largely taken up with public exercises. He is preaching and teaching, he is leading and praying and counseling. In fact, the minister cannot faithfully perform the duties of his office without sometimes "practicing his righteousness before men." But the sin does not lie here; it lies in the purpose clause that is attached. "Beware of practicing your righteousness before men, with the purpose that you might be noticed by them. Paul seemed to have comprehended this, so he wrote, "But as we were allowed of God to be put in trust with the gospel, even so we speak; not as pleasing men, but God, which trieth our hearts. For neither at any time used we flattering words, as ye know, nor a cloke of covetous-ness; God is witness: Nor of men sought we glory, neither of you, nor yet of others, when we might have been burdensome, as the apostles of Christ" **(1 Thessalonians 2:4-6).**

Those who would avoid Pastoral vainglory must understand the manner in which they are to lead. Peter tells us we are not to be lords over the flocks because they are God's heritage; instead we should lead by examples **(1 Peter 5:3).**

**The purpose of ministry is to express elements of God's character through human hands and lips.** It is a real challenge to do that when you have not subscribed to those elements yourself. Constantly metering and inspecting your motives and expressions will help you to avoid these and other pitfalls that many minister leaders fall into. We are human, no doubt. But, God does not ever use our humanity as an excuse for pride, arrogance, faithlessness, fear, or ambition. As we strip away our own attitudes and perspectives, we gain the mind of Christ.

Before you know it, we say things like "I am anointed. I am the owner and founder of this my big ministry. Millions of people watch me on TV. I am a multi-millionaire. I can buy anything and everything I want. God has blessed me and set me up high. It's true that other people must obey certain rules. But I am above that." When a man of God starts to think this way, it is the beginning of a fall. **Proverbs 16:18** says that, "Pride goeth before destruction and a haughty spirit before a fall." May we not fall away from God's Grace in Jesus name. May the power of God continue to accompany us, direct our part, and give us wisdom, discernment of spirit to avoid every set traps and loopholes in Jesus name. Amen

In the world today, we have many Potiphar's wives around. People whose basic mission on earth is to bring down men and women of God: and destroy work that God's people have been building for many years.

# CHAPTER TWO

## The Hidden Trap of Women

Many Christians are ensnared in the sex trap. This is second hidden trap organized by the devil. It is true that God created sex for the enjoyment of men and women in the context of marriage and for procreation, but the sins of fornication and adultery are weakening the fabric of the Body of Christ and diminishing its witness. Many are falling into the sex trap because they are seeking love in all the wrong places rather than submitting themselves to God. **1 Thessalonians 4:3 says that, "For this is the will of God, your sanctification: that you should abstain from sexual immorality,"** Sexual immorality can hinder Christians from being all they can be in God.

### How Joseph Escapes the Sex Trap

Throughout the history of mankind, Satan has used beautiful women and handsome men to do his handiwork. No one is immune from Satan's dirty tricks. If you let down your defenses and become weak in any way, you have just opened the door for Satan to walk in. Being a Christian makes you his number one prospect. He is an enemy of God, and he hates it when he loses you to God. Satan wants you to always remain in his kingdom, so he can use you against God's people.

Now let us look at the story of Joseph, who was an honorable man. He was handsome in form of appearance. He was the eleventh son of Jacob and his ten older brothers hated him because he was their father's favorite son. Joseph was very different from his brothers. He was quiet and thoughtful, well behaved and polite. His brothers were rough and ill-mannered, often disobedient and careless in the duties of worship. Joseph was a dreamer and he was unwise enough to tell his brothers of his dreams and that made them very angry.

It was only natural that a boy with a quick mind and a lively imagination should dream of glorious days to come in the future, but his brothers could not understand his dreams and hopes.

There were two dreams in particular which added to the envy and hatred of Joseph's brothers. In the first he dreamt that he and his brothers were binding sheaves of wheat in the field and that his sheaf suddenly stood upright, while the sheaves of his brothers bowed before it. In the other dream he saw the sun, and eleven stars also bowed before him.

His brothers thought that Joseph was telling them these dreams because he expected some day to rule over them. They disliked him very much for having such hopes and for even suggesting that he might become the head of his father's household.

They disliked Joseph so much that they began to plot among themselves what they might do to dispose of him. One of the brothers suggested that they slay him and put his body in a well in the field and then they could tell their father that Joseph had been killed and eaten by a wild animal.

The envy of these wicked brothers had grown into such bitter hatred that they did not stop even at the thought of murder. Because they knew that their brother was better than them, they were willing to commit the awful crime of murder to stop his dream.

God did not allow them to murder Joseph, so he sent a caravan of Ish'ma-el-ites their way. These people were slave traders and were on their way to Egypt. An older brother named Judah suggested that instead of leaving Joseph in the pit to die, they could sell him to these slave traders and they would get rid of him for good. The Ish'ma-el-ites took Joseph into Egypt here they sold him to a man named Pot'I-phar as a house hold servant (**Genesis 37:1-3).** Potiphar was a high officer in the army of Pharaoh. Even though he was a slave, Joseph did not give up hope that someday his dreams would come true.

Through his ups and downs, Joseph always trusted God, would help him through even the most difficult circumstances. Joseph was pleasant and cheerful by nature and blessed with a quick mind and upright heart. He did his work so well in the house of Potiphar that he won the complete trust of his master and was rapidly promoted to positions of greater honor. Eventually, Potiphar made Joseph his chief steward, giving him control of his entire household. Though Potiphar did not worship the God of Joseph, he was greatly impressed by the good character and true faith of his servant.

Honoring God he was now being honored by the Lord he worshipped, having served faithfully, he was now made the **"ruler over many…"** having learned to manage Potiphar's house, he was now preparing to rule over all the land of Egypt.

But Satan didn't like that he was honoring God versus him. He had something better in mind instead. So he presented Potiphar's wife to Joseph. She was immediately attracted by his magnetic personality and manliness and sought to lure him into a friendship. Joseph wished to maintain the integrity of his character and good opinion of his master, and was careful not to do anything to violate the trust bestowed on him. But once a woman sets her eyes on you and her deter-mines that you are truly what she wants, she will not stop until she has her hooks on you. He listened to her pleas. "Joseph come and lies with me." But he refused and said to his master's wife, "Look my master does not know what is with me in the house, and he hath committed all that he hath to my hand; There is none greater in this house than I nor has he kept back anything from me but you, because you are his wife. **How then can I do this great wickedness and sin against God?** So it was, as she spoke to Joseph day by day that he did not heed her, to lie with her or to be with her" **(Genesis 39:8-10).**

Now here's a woman who has been scorned and totally rejected by the man she desires; when you reject a woman like this one, be prepared to pay a very high price. There are many innocent men in prison today for the crime of rejecting a heart broken woman.

Today, Satan and his agents are still going about deceiving and destroying people, especially if you refuse to commit sin with them. They go ahead and send evil reports about you to all who knows you, even in church. They twist the story, and tell lies about you. Just like Potiphar's wife; they will get punished one day as the truth unveils by the Grace of God.

The Lord will expose them and destroy them completely. If you said no to the unwanted sexual advance, but your enemy wants to destroy you, do not worry. Leave it in God's hands because one day the tables will be turned and God Almighty will vindicate you.

However, this woman was not through with Joseph yet. He does not know what is in store for him. The next time Joseph is in the house alone, she comes in to him and once again pleads with Joseph to lie with her. When Joseph refuses this beautiful woman ripped her dress open and began to scream at the top of her voice. Rape, rape, this man has tried to rape me. She grabbed Joseph's garment, and he ran outside into the court yard with nothing on. Now Satan has really gone big with this one. He has a good man just where he wants him with no way out. Joseph seems to have been caught in the act. No

DNA test is available to prove his innocence. He is cast into prison where the king's other servants are detained. Nevertheless, the Lord was with Joseph and showed him mercy and gave him favor with the keeper of the prison. God always provides a way of escape for his people.

Satan used Potiphar's wife, a very beautiful woman to set the trap for Joseph. Only Joseph would not succumb to Satan's evil ways and for that, he was put into prison for a crime he did not commit.

While in prison, Joseph was found faithful, dedicated, trusting in the Lord God. He was encouraging to those who were hopeless and depressed in prison. He encouraged them daily.

There is a Christian movie titled: **"One careless night."** A careless night could end our ministries and all we have worked for. A careless night could bring an end to our labor for our families. A careless night could bring sorrow to anyone who does not take heed.

In the world today, we have many Potiphar's wives around. People whose basic mission on earth is to bring down men and women of God: and destroy work that God's people have been building for many years.

Men and women of God must be careful in the ministry and in every aspect of life. May God give us the spirit of revelation and discernment to see things before they happen.

The world is also full of Jezebels, people who think they can lie on a man or woman of God, then turn around to ask for a settlement of thousands of dollars. What they forget is that the leprosy of Miriam is still around today. No liar will go unpunished. Either now or later, everything shall come to light.

Most spiritual leaders stumble because they think themselves strong, but are not "strong in the grace that is in Christ Jesus" **(2 Timothy 2:1).**

# CHAPTER THREE

## THE HIDDEN TRAP OF MONEY

The third trap we must beware of is money. Money is good and necessary for the expansion of the Kingdom of God. The Bible even says in **Ecclesiastes 10:19a, "feast is made for laughter, and wine maketh merry: but money answereth all things."**

Also the Bible says about money in: **1 Timothy 6:10, "For the love of money is the root of all evil: which while some coveted after, they have erred from the faith, and pierced themselves through with many sorrows."**

But some scandalous sin destroys the white garment of integrity so badly that the reproach remains long after the sin has been forgiven and properly forgotten. Satan knows this, and wages efficient warfare on God's church by targeting pastors and prominent men and women of the faith. In so doing, each blow has the simultaneous effect of four: Satan marginalizes God's children (who he sees as enemies; **(1 Timothy 3:2)**, makes them compromise **(Acts. 20:28; Tit. 1:9); demoralizes** them through betrayal, and worst of all, tempt them with occasions to blaspheme **(2 Samuel 12:14).**

Most spiritual leaders stumble because they think themselves strong, but are not "strong in the grace that is in Christ Jesus" **(2 Timothy 2:1).** Thinking they can stand, and failing to take heed, they fall **(1 Cor. 10:12).** But when a pastor takes a bullet, the whole church bleeds. And so pastors must be vigilant. With this in mind, we'll devote the next few chapters to taking heed about the three most common traps laid for spiritual leaders: money, glory, and women.

It is good to face temptation and prevail. But better not to encounter temptation in the first place. After all, Jesus taught us to pray, "Lead us not into temptation" **(Matthew 6:13).** But the naivetés with which many pastors handle financial temptation invokes images of a cheeky white boy taking a midnight stroll through the back alleys of Harlem--they're begging for a beating. So the following are some suggestions that might help pastors and their churches to wise up.

**The first way, is to avoid financial temptation -** As a man of God is simply to live within your means. Make a budget and stick to it. Avoid debt --it is a form of slavery that divides your loyalties between two masters. Live in a house you can afford. Buy a car you can afford. Furthermore build a church you and your congregation can afford. When our first church was about to be built, due to lack of experience and other reasons, we planned for a 10,000 sq. ft. building. In the end, we realized we could not afford this and reduced it to about 5000 sq.ft. Our mortgage for the first three years was two thousand four hundred and forty eight dollars and eighty –four cents every month. As of today, thank God we are paying three thousand three hundred dollars every month. This is far better than renting.

**Proverbs 16:8, "Better is a little with righteous-ness than great revenues without right."**

So when considering a purchase, distinguish between that which meets real needs, and that which meets a want. When in doubt about how to manage your finances consult your accountant. Integrity is a very fragile thing.

Secondly, practice generous giving. Not only is this a good model for the flock, but it also keeps your eyes where they belong--on a self-existent God who doesn't need your money, and who Himself gives to all creatures their portion (**Acts 17:24-25; Matthew 6:19-34).** So focus on God to meet all your needs; since He is the one that called you, He will meet your needs according to His riches in glory by Christ Jesus. In our own case, we are a great testimony to the goodness of God. I had to settle for an IT job with the Government, so I wouldn't have to travel on my job; until the Lord asked me to go into full time ministry. So, in the year 2007, I resigned from my well paying job that I loved so dearly, but thank God today I can testify that God is faithful. It was challenging and still is, but we serve a mighty God who is my provider and will always be in Jesus name.

Let us address what churches can do to help their pastors avoid financial temptation. Churches must look to their pastors to model fiscal godliness. This presupposes, of course, that pastors have finances to manage. Many churches embrace the devil's adage, **"We'll keep him poor, and God will keep him humble."** But this opens wide the door to temptation. When a man sees his children hungry and the desk piled with bills, filching a loaf from the Safeway doesn't seem all that wrong. But Jesus said **"a worker is worthy of His wages" (1 Timothy 5:18),** and **the previous verse exhorts the church to pay teaching elders double (1 Tim. 5:17).** Out of this they will be able to feed and educate their families and children, provide for their later less-productive years, show hospitality, and give generously.

Thirdly, keep your pastor away from the money. The pastor should never touch the offering, except to put something into it. Nor should he be given a clue that the Smiths are loaded but never tithe, and the Johnsons are not, but give sacrificially (**James 2:1**). Instead, **elders and deacons** should handle the money, deposit checks, etc. Similarly, the pastor should not be given signing authority on any accounts if it can be avoided. One cannot be accused of mishandling funds to which he has no access. Though, this may not be possible in a small church where the Pastors don't have deacons to help, not even in-house accountant. Where the pastor was not hired, he or she should not totally close his eyes to the account of the ministry.

The fourth way to protect your pastor from temptation is to require him or her to have an open door policy in regard to every transaction made on behalf of the church by validating all expenses. Don't be timid or shy about asking respectfully pointed questions of him. Extra paperwork and pointed questions may seem like a hassle, but the process will yield good results in the end.

A good Pastor and a good teacher will feed believers with healthy teaching (good, wholesome food from the Word of God).

# CHAPTER FOUR

## The Hidden Trap of Internal Enemy

From within we are faced with enemies as well. We have those who are corrupting the church and spreading strife and division by disregarding the precepts and principles set forth by Christ to govern and regulate his people. Jesus said, **"Whosoever therefore shall break one of these least command-ments and shall teach men so, shall be called least in the kingdom of heaven"** **(Matthew 5:19).**

These brethren hold a faulty attitude about the faith. It is known as legalism. The legalists are spiritual grandchildren of the Pharisees of Jesus' day. They profess a great love for the law of God and his church, but they have little love for the people of God. They are quick to divide the body, and place a low premium on the unity of the church. They often delight more in going to war against fellow preachers than in fighting against the true enemies of the church, they are to the church as bounty hunters are to the law. **They discourage weak members and drive them away.** Liberals are grateful for legalists. They hold them up as examples of all that is wrong in the church and imply that all who do not buy their package of change are like them.

# FIRST ENEMY - DIVISION

1 Corinthians 1: 10, "Now I beseech you, brethren, by the name of our Lord Jesus Christ, that ye all speak the same thing, and that there be no divisions among you; but that ye be perfectly joined together in the same mind and in the same judgment."

[11]For it hath been declared unto me of you, my brethren, by them which are of the house of Chloe, that there are contentions among you.

[12]Now this I say, that every one of you saith, I am of Paul; and me of Apollos; and me of Cephas; and me of Christ.

These Christians were getting together and forming different groups within the church and each group thought they were better than the other group!

It is a terrible thing to see family warfare within the church. It is a terrible thing to see gossip, jealousy, pride, failure to love the brethren, etc. Such things cause division and harm. Christians sometimes are so busy fighting each other that they have little time or energy left to battle the real enemies: the world, the flesh and the devil! How are Christians supposed to live with each other (see **Ephesians 4:2-3; 31-32).**

# SECOND ENEMY – CLOSED BIBLE

One of the great enemies that the church faces today is the closed Bible. There are many churches where the Bible is used very little. The next time you see people walking to church see if they are carrying their Bibles. There are many people today who do not even bring a Bible of any kind to church. There are many Pastors who never encourage their people to open their Bibles and use them (by turning to different passages). In many churches the Bible is a closed Book. It should not be so.

**Let us go to the Word of God for a moment.**

# PROVERBS 4: 20-22

[20]My son, attend to my Words; incline thine ear unto my sayings.

[21]Let them not depart from thine eyes; keep them in the midst of thine heart.

[22]For they are life unto those that find them, and health to all their flesh

# PSALM 119

vs. 105, "Thy word is a lamp unto my feet, and a light unto my path."

vs. 130, "The entrance of thy words giveth light; it giveth understanding unto the simple."

vs. 133, "Order my steps in thy word: and let not any iniquity have dominion over me."

vs. 139, "My zeal hath consumed me, because mine enemies have forgotten thy words."

vs. 140, "Thy word is very pure: therefore thy servant loveth it."

The Word of God is so important in our lives that we cannot do without it. Many Christians do not bring their Bible to church anymore because of the dis-played screens. They think, oh they will show it on the screen on Sunday. A Christian who hates to read the Word of God will soon be a dead Christian.

# THIRD ENEMY - EMOTIONALISM

Emotionalism is a problem when people are led by their feelings and emotions (being glad, sad, angry, etc.) instead of being led by God's Word.

Most people are led and controlled by their feelings and emotions. When asked, "Why did you do that?" the common answer is, "Because I felt like it!" Feelings do not do very well in the driver's seat. Feelings come and feelings go. Feelings change and fluctuate. Bad feelings should point to the true problem, which is what causes the feelings. Usually the real problem has to do with the way a person lives. Bad feelings are usually the result of bad living or bad thinking. When the warning light flashes on your car's dashboard, it is telling you that there is a problem under the hood. Our feelings are like this flashing light.

Martin Luther once said: "For feelings come and feelings go, and feelings are deceiving. My warrant is the Word of God, naught else is worth believing." God's unchanging Word must lead us and guide us. How I feel is not important. The important thing is this: What has God said?

There are many churches today that are swept up in emotionalism. If you were to walk into one of these churches, you would see some very strange things: arms waving in the air, people making strange sounds which do not make any sense, different people speaking at the same time, and all kinds of movement and excitement. But in the middle of all this move-ment and excitement the Bible stays closed. The people do not stay quiet and still long enough for the Lord to speak to their hearts through His Word (**Study 1 Kings 19:11–12; Isaiah 49).**

# FOURTH ENEMY - WORLDLINESS

Unsaved people are of the world because they belong to Satan's system. The devil wants to draw believers away from the Savior, and to draw them close to the world.

Consider **Romans 12:2,** Jesus wants to transform us (change us by working in our hearts), but Satan wants to conform us (squeeze us into the world's mold). For example, think about the kind of language that many of our classmates may use at school. They may use bad language, swear, make fun of others, and tell dirty jokes. As a believer and as a member of the Church, you do not want to conform your language to theirs by allowing the same kind of filth to come out of your mouth. Instead you want the Savior to transform your language so that you can enjoy the healthy use of your mind. Then unbelievers will be able to see that the language a Christian uses is good, and wholesome and different. **"Let no corrupt (filthy) communication proceed out of your mouth"(Ephesians 4:29).** Don't let garbage come out of your mouth. Rather, speak the kind of language that will encourage and build up others (see the end of verse 29).

The worldly person is the person who ignores God and who leaves God out of his thinking. He does not consider God in his thoughts, his plans, or his actions. He lives as if there were no God in heaven. The average person does not give God very much thought during the day. The Christian believer must be different! God is at the very center of his life, and he must include God in all of his thinking and plans and actions. When we live this way we are being a good witness, because we are causing others to realize that there is a God in heaven.

What does God think about worldliness (**1 John 2:15-17 and James 4:4**)? The more the Church becomes like the world, the more it will lose its witness and its power. Unsaved people will say, "Why do I need to become a Christian? The Christians that I know are no different than my other friends. They act like non-Christians, they talk like non-Christians, they think like non-Christians and I can't tell much of a difference. If Christians are no different than non-Christians, then why should I become a Christian?".

# FIFTH ENEMY - FALSE TEACHING

Did you know that there are people today going around and poisoning men's souls? Just as the body needs to be fed with healthy food, so the soul needs to be fed with healthy teaching. The Bible calls healthy teaching sound doctrine (**Titus 2:1**). A good Pastor and a good teacher will feed believers with healthy teaching (good, wholesome food from the Word of God). A false teacher will feed people with false teaching (poison).

Where and how do false teachers do their work? Some speak on the radio or appear on television. Some write articles in magazines, books, the Internet. Some false teachers stand behind pulpits and teach people in churches. Some false teachers go from house to house and from door to door trying to talk to people and spread their lies. Some false teachers are sincere and they really think that they are helping people, but they are sincerely wrong. They are deceived (**2 Tim. 3:13**).

## Some examples of false teachings:

1.  Once saved, always saved even if you commit sin and live in it.
2.  To be saved, a person must keep the Ten Commandment
3.  You must pray through Mary the Mother of Jesus

4.  Jesus Christ is the greatest angel that God ever created
5.  Such a loving father will never punish people in hell

## SIXTH ENEMY - INTERNAL HUMAN BUGS

A bug is a spy device for listening to someone's conversation. Humans around the church act like this device. They are rumor carriers that have broken up many families and Churches. They almost broke ours too.

If they are ministers, every minute of the meetings would be relayed to the enemies of the church, or the Pastor in order to cause division. Most of these human bugs are not really saved or they have been bought by the enemy of the Kingdom of God for 30 pieces of silver. The end of this is always regretted.

They are not in church for the benefit of the church. They hang around, work hard, and devote their time and gifts, only to break down the church later. These kinds of people must be noticed and never placed in any position of authority. They must not be involved in the Board, Trustees, or Minister Groups.

If you are a bug in any ministry, please change because you are only fighting God and not man. And trust me, from Genesis to Revelation, from generation to generation; no man has ever won any battle against God. You will fail no matter what. It is just a matter of time. There is no peace for the wicked says the Lord.

So the very best thing is to repent and surrender to God, who can kill and give life.

There are also Christians who are not bugs, but are careless. Careless Christians are being used by the enemies of the kingdom today. Some don't have their own minds. They follow just anyone. They do not want to offend friends even though they know they are treading the way of destruction.

Brethren, you need to base your decisions on the Word of God. Understand that friends come, friends go, and the only one who will never leave you is Jesus Christ.

# CHAPTER FIVE

## THE HIDDEN TRAP OF THE EXTERNAL ENEMY

While on earth, Christ was confronted with enemies who wished to destroy him and defeat his mission. Having conquered death and ascended back to the Father, he left his church on earth to spread the message of salvation to the world for which he died **(Mark 16:15).** From her inception, the Church of Christ has been besieged by enemies within and without. Paul and his helpers were harassed by hostile Jews and angry Gentiles who resorted to violence to silence the great missionary.

The disciples also had to cope with opposition from misguided Christians. Some Jewish disciples devoted themselves to harassing the apostles and imposing their Jewish customs on Gentile converts. Listen to his plaintiff words, "Our flesh had no rest, but we were troubled on every side; without were fighting's, within were fears.." **(2 Corinthians7:5).** Others corrupted the faith and led disciples astray with teaching that was contrary to the divine's message of Christ **(2 Timothy1:15).** Today the church of Christ is besieged by foes both within and without. From without we are under attack by:

- a hostile culture,
- militant unbelief,
- pagan religions,

- hundreds of counterfeit churches,
- an antagonistic media.

These enemies alone are enough to occupy every soldier of Christ in a never ending struggle with the forces of evil.

Thus contemporary soldiers of Christ stand with their backs to the wall, trying to fend off two enemies at the same time, while legalistic brethren are snapping at their heels like snarling dogs. Satan is shrewd. He knows that every hour soldiers of Christ spend fighting enemies within and without is time lost for evangelizing and saving lost souls (**Rev. 19:11-21**). Those vanquished will drink the bitter cup of wrath on the Day of Judgment, whether they are enemies within or enemies without.

**Revelation 19:11-21:** [11] And I saw heaven opened, and behold a white horse; and he that sat upon him was called Faithful and true, and in righteousness he doth judge and make war.

[12] His eyes were as a flame of fire, and on his head were many crowns; and he had a name written, that no man knew, but he himself.

[13] And he was clothed with vesture dipped in blood: and his name is called The Word of God.

[14] And the armies which were in heaven followed him upon white horses, clothed in fine linen, white and clean.

[15] And out of his mouth goeth a sharp sword, that with it he should smite the nations: and he shall rule them with a rod of iron: and he treadeth the winepress of the fierceness and wrath of Almighty God.

[16] And he hath on his vesture and on his thigh a name written, KING OF KINGS, AND LORD OF LORDS.

<sup>17</sup> And I saw an angel standing in the sun; and he cried with a loud voice, saying to all the fowls that fly in the midst of heaven, Come and gather yourselves together unto the supper of the great God;

<sup>18</sup> That ye may eat the flesh of kings, and the flesh of captains, and the flesh of mighty men, and the flesh of horses, and of them that sit on them, and the flesh of all men, both free and bond, both small and great.

<sup>19</sup> And I saw the beast, and the kings of the earth, and their armies, gathered together to make war against him that sat on the horse, and against his army.

<sup>20</sup> And the beast was taken, and with him the false prophet that wrought miracles before him, with which he deceived them that had received the mark of the beast, and them that worshipped his image. These both were cast alive into a lake of fire burning with brimstone.

<sup>21</sup> And the remnants were slain with the sword of him that sat upon the horse, which sword proceeded out of his mouth: and all the fowls were filled with their flesh.

# CHAPTER SIX

## The Hidden Trap of Jealousy

"Jealousy" is resenting the fact that others have some thing, do something, or are something that you wish you had, could do, or were.

**James 3:14, 16, "But if ye have bitter envying and strife in your hearts, glory not, and lie not against the truth. (vs. 16), for where envying and strife is, there is confusion and every evil work.**

If jealousy is not repented from, and if you're suffering from that sin, and you don't deal with it, you don't let God deal with it in your heart, then jealousy is going to turn to hate. That hate will wind up consuming your entire life, it will control you.

And so jealousy can control you if you don't let God deal with it. Do you harbor jealousy towards anyone at work? In your community? In the church or even in your own family? I've discovered people who claim to love Christ can have jealousy toward members of their family. So how do you put an end to jealousy?

First of all, you need to start thanking God for what you have, who you are, and what you can do, because if you don't you are not going to be anything, you are not going to accomplish anything for God, because your mind is on other people too much. Start thanking God for other people, in fact it wouldn't hurt to go up to someone that you tend to have jealousy towards and say "I thank God for you," and mean it in your heart. You can continue by saying, I am thankful for your gifts, for your abilities, for your position, and I'm going to pray for you and encourage you in any way I can." I'm not telling you to be a hypocrite but after much prayer and after God have dealt with you, and then you can do that with a pure and clear conscience. So don't let jealousy control you, it will rob you."

Do you realize that if any of the people you are pray-ing for have a strong ministry or family, you will become a part of that ministry and not an enemy of it!

# RECOGNIZING JEALOUSY

If we are to put to death this vile sin, then we must know some signs of its existence in our lives. Knowing we possess a certain negative trait is half the battle won toward eliminating it. Here are some questions and statements to deal with if you believe you have envy toward anyone. Let's call the people we envy Brother& Sister Stone or Thomas.

I must be a hypocrite when Brother Stone is present!

On the outside I am as sweet as ever, but inside is something else. I am acting like I really like him when I am, in reality, jealous of him in every way. We see this in our Churches today.

I am preoccupied with the things Sister Stone has!

I know the Bible tells us to look upon the things of others in **Philippians 2:4** but that does not mean we should dwell on their goods or covet them. When we find ourselves consistently thinking about the things of others, it is a sure sign of jealousy.

### I question why God has given Mr. Stone so much and I have so little!

When you begin to make inquiries about why one person has so much more than you, it is another sure sign that you are jealous of them. This also applies to covetousness in the mind. One need not reveal how jealous they are verbally, because sins of the mind are equal to sins of deed with God. You can detect envy in a statement like, "If I had his money, I would surely give much more to the church."

### You borrow to buy something you can't afford!

Now the people in this category don't have children or have one or two, so they do not need large home. I am not speaking of a necessity such as a car or home but I am speaking of the items of luxury you see in Sister Stone's home, car, etc. and you try to outdo her by buying a better set than hers.

### You pre-judge the motives of Mrs. Stone

When Sister Stone does something nice we tend to judge her motives through our envious eyes. When ever we view another person through our envy, we are secretly or openly assassinating their character. Even if Sister Stone does do things for the wrong reason, she is accountable to the Lord and not us.

### We blame God for blessing Brother Stone

When we envy Brother Stone, we keep asking the question over and over again, why does God keep blessing him the way He does? Brothers and Sisters that is God's business! If you believe God has made a mistake, then tell Him that you should be receiving those blessings, but do not be surprised if God blesses Brother Stone more in response to your request. You see, God does not answer sinful requests.

DR. TAI OLAMIGOKE

## We find ourselves gossiping about Brother Stone

The more we find ourselves dwelling on the things of others, the more we tend to gossip about them. Since gossip is normally rooted in a created scenario, our minds will invent situations and scenarios that we will believe about Sister Stone, and we will actually believe them, and pass them on. By the time the gossip is all over the church, Sister Stone's reputation is ruined, but so is the reputation of the person who started the rumor.

Whenever you have a desire to say something about someone, check your motives, and then check your tongue, and then check in with Heaven for forgiveness for allowing Satan to motivate you this far.

## We may have a hidden desire to see adversity come into the life of Brother Stone

Have you ever said or heard it said, "I wonder how they would act if they were going through what I am experiencing? This statement tends to have a little jealousy behind it as we believe Brother Stone has been living a good life without any problems. We never know what others experience out of our sight. Most people we think are having a good life may actually be struggling. We look at what people have to judge whether they are doing alright or not.

I believe these guidelines are sufficient to open our eyes to this sin. If you had any of these situations in your life then maybe God is raising your attention so you can purge that sin and begin to reclaim your mind for Christ.

Now I wish to help you deal with envy, to see you free in your Christian walk. **Envy is a great hindrance to Christian growth.** Do you realize that you will progress no further in your spiritual life than the sin that is besetting you? You may gain knowledge but

CHRISTIAN AND LEADERSHIP HIDDEN TRAPS TO AVOID

knowledge is not spiritual growth! Once the besetting sin is removed, you will grow again. I pray that you will grow again in Jesus' name.

# DEALING WITH JEALOUSY

Once we discover the root of jealousy in our life, we may proceed to deal with it so we may reclaim our spiritual walk without any of the weight that besets us as stated in **Hebrews 12:1,** "Wherefore seeing we also are compassed about with so great a cloud of witnesses, let us lay aside every weight, and the sin which doth so easily beset us, and let us run with patience the race that is set before us."

## 1. ADMIT IT TO THE LORD!

The Bible teaches in Proverbs 28:13 that, "**He that covereth his sins shall not prosper: but whosoever confesseth and forsaketh them shall have mercy.**"

IF YOU HAVE VERBALLY OFFENDED THE ONE YOU ENVY, ADMIT IT TO THEM. IF NOT, DEAL WITH IT PRIVATELY OR WITH ANOTHER FRIEND WHO WILL NOT JUSTIFY YOUR SIN.

**Matthew 18:15** says that, "Moreover if thy brother shall trespass against thee, go and tell him his fault between thee and him alone: if he shall hear thee, thou hast gained thy brother."

If jealousy is in your mind, then deal with it without making the person aware of your jealousy. At a future time you may wish to tell that person, but wait until it is all out of your system. If you tell them, they may be shocked that someone is jealous of them, and a new friendship may start.

## 2. LEARN THE PRINCIPLES OF COMMITMENT

Paul lays these principles out for us in Philippians 4:11-13 and they should be dissected and digested. Here are three that should suffice in getting you on the right tract.

**Philippians 4:11-13, "Not** that I speak in respect of want: for I have learned, in whatsoever state I am, therewith to be content. vs.12, I know both how to be abased, and I know how to abound: everywhere and in all things I am instructed both to be full and to be hungry, both to abound and to suffer need. vs. 13, I can do all things through Christ which strengtheneth me."

## A. Be Satisfied with what you have

You do not need any more than God has supplied for you at this moment in time. Where we get into trouble is we think we need something when in essence we want something. To further strengthen that indictment, we go for more credit cards to fulfill our desires while withholding the fact that credit cards can ruin us financially. The proper use of credit cards are not sins, the abuse of them are.

A few years ago, my wife and I decided to pay off our credit cards. My only card was paid off, cut up and we lived within our means. Just this year I got another one because of ministry travels. I make sure I pay off what I use each month before the due date. I also make sure to pay more than the minimum payment. So if you can manage your credit card, get one instead of five. Do not use credit cards to buy people Christmas gifts, thinking you will pay say $5000 off after January. It may not happen.

## B. God allows you to be Strong in One Area but Lacking in Another.

God allows us to be in want, in some areas for the purpose of keeping us faithful to Him. If He gave us everything we wanted, how many

of us would live to be 70? "He, who has ears to hear, let him hear."
God If He gave us everything we wanted how many of us want to
fellowship with Him and come to Him with both praise and needs.

## C. Contentment Is Learning To Trust God In Your Present Situation!

Contentment is learning to trust God completely. It is easy to thank
God when He has abundantly blessed us; but to thank God for areas of
need is another story. When Joseph was placed in prison, he learned to
trust God through his ordeal and the outcome was promotion.

**Someone's answer to Jealousy:** God is a jealous God. He wants no
other gods put before him. This may sound petty but He did create
us after all. Jealousy among men is a sin. If a man is jealous of another
man because of things he has, it can lead to all kinds of problems.
Stealing, hate, killing etc. "Thou shall not covet another man's wife"
or his lawn mower or his life or anything that belongs to him.

Jealousy has led to murder. Don't desire what some one else has. You
may not want the whole package.

People see a family and think, **"They have it good."** "They really
love each other." Yes they do on the outside, but you do not know the
challenges they are going through. And so for someone to be jealous of
them or wishing that they have their kind of life would be a mistake.
Don't be jealous of anybody or family. Thank the Lord for every day
that you have together. The Lord wants us to be thankful for everything.

The Devil tries to tell us there will not be a penalty for disobedience. He tries to entrap us to get us to believe that there will not be consequences for any form of disobedience.

# CHAPTER SEVEN

## THE HIDDEN TRAP OF LIES

The enemy (Satan) uses lies to create doubt, and to lure us into his trap. In the book of Genesis, the Devil in the form of a serpent created doubt in the mind of Eve by saying, "Did God really say? (Genesis 3:1).

His opening move pulled mankind into sin and rebel-ion against God, and he wants to create doubt through lies and distortions of the truth that he is trying to get Eve to believe.

**In the book of Matthew 4:3**, Jesus is being tempted in the same way. *"If thou be the Son of God."*

First the Devil raises doubt, then he sends the temptat-ion to try to lead us astray, and his tactics have not changed. He seeks to get us to ignore the great blessings that come from a relationship with God, or the riches of Christian marriage and family, the security of a Christian home, the level of friendship that we can enjoy as Christians, and countless other things that God offers to those who know and love the Lord. He seeks to entrap us into thinking and concentrating on a tiny list of prohibitions of what Christians are not allowed to do. There are very few things that God does not allow us to do, and there are very good reasons why He prohibits those things.

In the case of Eve, the Devil said to her that God was keeping them from something that was very desirable. In this case, it was for them to be like God and knowing the difference between good and evil **(Genesis 3:5).** Satan tries to make God look like who does not want what's best for our lives. He tries to make us think we are really missing out on life by obeying God. The Devil tries to tell us there will not be a penalty for disobedience. He tries to entrap us to get us to believe that there will not be consequences for any form of disobedience.

Like Eve in Genesis 3:4, he says to us, *"You will not surely die."* He says in effect that it won't hurt you, or do any harm if you disobey God. But the very truth is that disobedience causes us to miss out on so much that God Almighty has in store for us to have in life.

## THE DEVIL'S FAVORITE ENTRAPMENT

God gave Adam and Eve a chance to repent. God said to them in Genesis **3:11,**"Who told you that you were naked? Did you eat fruit from the tree I commanded you not to eat from?"

Instead of repenting they blamed; did you eat fruit from the tree I commanded you not to eat from?" The man answered, "That woman, the one you gave me, gave me some fruit from the tree, and I ate it."Then the LORD God asked the woman, "What have you done? ""The snake deceived me, and I ate," the woman answered (Genesis 3:11-13). We can't blame each other or even the devil when we sin.

**James 1:13-15, "When tempted, no one should say, "God is tempting me. For God cannot be tempted by evil, nor does he tempt anyone; vs. 14, but each one is tempted when, by his own evil desire, he is dragged away and enticed. vs. 15,**

then, after desire has conceived, it gives birth to sin; and sin, when it is full-grown, gives birth to death."

The Devil uses lies to lead us to doubt, then he tells us we are missing out because Gods boundaries of conduct are so restrictive and that we are missing out. Then the Devil cons us into believing that there will be no consequences for our disobedience, and then he tries to get us to blame everyone else for our sins.

**1 John 1:9 says that, if we just admit that we have sinned, then God will forgive us and cleanse us from all unrighteousness.**

God wants us to know that even if we fall into one of the traps of the enemy, He will always be "a very present help in time of trouble" and in time of our need. He also does not want us to be ignorant of the Devil's devices that he uses to try to entrap us. This is not a license to commit sin because God's standard is holiness.

**1 John 4:4 says, "You are from God, little children, and have overcome them; because these things to you so that you may not sin. And if anyone sins, we have an Advocate with the Father greater is He who is in you than he who is in the world." Amen**

**1 John 2:1 says, "My little children, I am writing, *Christ the* Jesus *righteous;"***

The above describes the devil as the father of all liars. If he is what the Bible calls him, it means that he has many children. And like the saying, 'like father like son', it means those children of his most definitely act like him. People lie to one another today because of one major thing "the love of money."

Repent, otherwise the Lord will fish you out once your cup is full. You cannot lie or run for ever. **Proverbs 28:1 says, "The wicked**

**flee when no man pursueth: but the righteous are bold as a lion."**

Liars can run from man, but not from God. The best solution is repentance because God has no pleasure in the death of sinners. You may think you are alive because you are still breathing. It is even better to die physically and go to Heaven instead of living and go to hell.

In those days and even today, Churches and Pastors settle with the enemy because of fear of their names being in the open. Whether you like it or not, in the end, your name will still be out there. Jesus name is still out there after 2000 years. People still talk bad about the Savior of the world whose main mission was to save those who were lost. He did this then and he is still is doing the same today. This is why a criminal can one day be saved, sanctified, and be called to preach the gospel.

All we must guide against is to make sure we live a life that pleases God, so when the enemy searches for things against us, he or she will not find anything.

**John 14:31says, "Hereafter I will not talk much with you: for the prince of this world cometh, and hath nothing in me."**

As long as you live right and you are relevant, the enemy of our faith will always come to try us. He will send his agents to our ministries, families, to try us, discourage and tempt us. We must always remember that greater is he that is in us than he that is in the world.

# CHAPTER EIGHT

## THE HIDDEN TRAP OF CARELESSNESS

Ministry today is more difficult than it has ever been. It seems that each day we hear of another colleague in ministry who has fallen into immorality, another who has burned out, another who has in some way weakened the credibility of those called to God's ministry. Why is this happening in record numbers today?

Perhaps amidst the hectic expectations that we encounter in "real" ministry, we lose sight of the commitments we made when we first accepted Christ our Lord and Savior. Perhaps the standards by which we promised to live when we followed His call to be His ministers have been overshadowed by exhaustion or carelessness. Whatever the cause, more and more in ministry are facing a crisis of integrity, righteous-ness, and credibility.

We are joined together by a common call from God to feed His sheep, but we are also tied by a common commitment to **purity, holiness, righteousness, and faithfulness.**

One thing I know is that society, cultures, and people changes, but the WORD of God remains the same from generation to generation.

The trap of carelessness in the ministry is caused by us and not the enemy most of the time.

# CARELESS CHURCH ONE: THE CHURCH AT EPHESUS

**Revelation 2:** [1]Unto the angel of the church of Ephesus write; These things saith he that holdeth the seven stars in his right hand, who walketh in the midst of the seven golden candlesticks;

[2]I know thy works, and thy labour, and thy patience, and how thou canst not bear them which are evil: and thou hast tried them which say they are apostles, and are not, and hast found them liars:

[3]And hast borne, and hast patience, and for my name's sake hast laboured, and hast not fainted.

[4]Nevertheless I have somewhat against thee, because thou hast left thy first love.

[5]Remember therefore from whence thou art fallen, and repent, and do the first works; or else I will come unto thee quickly, and will remove thy candlestick out of his place, except thou repent.

[6]But this thou hast, that thou hatest the deeds of the Nicolaitanes, which I also hate.

[7]He that hath an ear let him hear what the Spirit saith unto the churches; to him that overcometh will I give to eat of the tree of life, which is in the midst of the paradise of God.

The Church at Ephesus left their first love or former devotion to God. Where is the zeal we had when we first met the Lord? We were there whenever the Church doors were opened for Bible study, Sunday school, and prayer meetings. Many leaders zeal dies gradually as they prosper in the ministry. May this not be the portion of the reader of this book in Jesus' powerful name.

# CARELESS CHURCH TWO: THE CHURCH AT PERGAMOS

**Revelation** 2: [12]And to the angel of the church in Pergamos write; these things saith he which hath the sharp sword with two edges;

[13]I know thy works, and where thou dwellest, even where Satan's seat is: and thou holdest fast my name, and hast not denied my faith, even in those days wherein Antipas was my faithful martyr, who was slain among you, where Satan dwelleth.

[14]But I have a few things against thee, because thou hast there them that hold the doctrine of Balaam, who taught Balac to cast a stumbling block before the children of Israel, to eat things sacrificed unto idols, and to commit fornication.

[15]So hast thou also them that hold the doctrine of the Nicolaitanes, which thing I hate.

[16]Repent; or else I will come unto thee quickly, and will fight against them with the sword of my mouth.

[17]He that hath an ear, let him hear what the Spirit saith unto the churches; to him that overcometh will I give to eat of the hidden manna, and will give him a white stone, and in the stone a new name written, which no man knoweth saving he that receiveth it.

This church was careless because they hold the doctrine of Balaam, who taught Balak to cast a stumbling block before the children of Israel, to eat things sacrificed unto idols, to commit fornication, and also to hold the doctrine of Nicolaitanes.

We must be careful not to deviate from the doctrine of Christ as we go into the ministry.

There is a time in everyone's life in the ministry when they get up there, and the devil will still wants us to twist, add, or remove ourselves from the word. Every Word we speak is very important, therefore, we must be careful about what we say when it comes to the Word of God.

## CHURCH THREE: CARELESS AT THE CHURCH THYATIRA

**Revelation 12:** [18]And unto the angel of the church in Thyatira write; these things saith the Son of God, who hath his eyes like unto a flame of fire, and his feet are like fine brass;

[19]I know thy works, and charity, and service, and faith, and thy patience, and thy works; and the last to be more than the first.

[20]Notwithstanding I have a few things against thee, because thou sufferest that woman Jezebel, which calleth herself a prophetess, to teach and to seduce my servants to commit fornication and to eat things sacrificed unto idols.

[21]And I gave her space to repent of her fornication; and she repented not.

[22]Behold, I will cast her into a bed, and them that commit adultery with her into great tribulation, except they repent of their deeds.

[23]And I will kill her children with death; and all the churches shall know that I am he who searcheth the reins and hearts: and I will give unto every one of you according to your works.

[24]But unto you I say, and unto the rest in Thyatira, as many as have not this doctrine, and which have not known the depths of Satan, as they speak; I will put upon you none other burden.

[25]But that which ye have already hold fast till I come.

[26]And he that overcometh, and keepeth my works unto the end, to him will I give power over the nations:

[27]And he shall rule them with a rod of iron; as the vessels of a potter shall they be broken to shivers: even as I received of my Father.

[28]And I will give him the morning star.

[29]He that hath an ear, let him hear what the Spirit saith unto the churches.

This church was careless because they allowed the woman called Jezebel which called herself prophetess to teach and to seduce the servants of God to commit fornication.

We must not allow anyone in the church leadership based on what they think they are, but on what God says they are. We must not harbor people because they are rich and self-important. God will take care of His church no matter what.

## CARELESS CHURCH FOUR: THE CHURCH AT SARDIS

**Revelation 3: 1-6:** [1]And unto the angel of the church in Sardis write; these things saith he that hath the seven Spirits of God, and the seven stars; I know thy works, that thou hast a name that thou livest, and art dead.

[2]Be watchful, and strengthen the things which remain, that are ready to die: for I have not found thy works perfect before God.

[3]Remember therefore how thou hast received and heard, and hold fast, and repent. If therefore thou shalt not watch, I will come on thee as a thief, and thou shalt not know what hour I will come upon thee.

[4]Thou hast a few names even in Sardis which have not defiled their garments; and they shall walk with me in white: for they are worthy.

[5]He that overcometh, the same shall be clothed in white raiment; and I will not blot out his name out of the book of life, but I will confess his name before my Father, and before his angels.

[6]He that hath an ear let him hear what the Spirit saith unto the churches.

## CARELESS CHURCH FIVE: THE CHURCH AT LAODICEA

**Revelation 3:14-22:** [14]And unto the angel of the church of the Laodiceans write; these things saith the Amen, the faithful and true witness, the beginning of the creation of God;

[15]I know thy works, that thou art neither cold nor hot: I would thou wert cold or hot.

[16]So then because thou art lukewarm, and neither cold nor hot, I will spue thee out of my mouth.

[17]Because thou sayest, I am rich, and increased with goods, and have need of nothing; and knowest not that thou art wretched, and miserable, and poor, and blind, and naked:

[18]I counsel thee to buy of me gold tried in the fire, that thou mayest be rich; and white raiment, that thou mayest be clothed, and that the shame of thy nakedness do not appear; and anoint thine eyes with eye salve, that thou mayest see.

[19]As many as I love, I rebuke and chasten: be zealous therefore, and repent.

²⁰Behold, I stand at the door, and knock: if any man hears my voice, and opens the door, I will come in to him, and will sup with him, and he with me.

²¹To him that overcometh will I grant to sit with me in my throne, even as I also overcame, and am set down with my Father in his throne.

²²He that hath an ear let him hear what the Spirit saith unto the churches.

This Church was careless because of Spiritual blindness. We must pray for the spirit of discernment in the ministry since the church has many types of people with different backgrounds.

# LET US LOOK AT WHAT GOD SAID ABOUT THE OTHER TWO CHURCHES

## 1. The Church at Smyrna

**Revelation 2: 8-1:** ⁸And unto the angel of the church in Smyrna write; these things saith the first and the last, which was dead, and is alive;

⁹I know thy works, and tribulation, and poverty, (but thou art rich) and I know the blasphemy of them which say they are Jews, and are not, but are the synagogue of Satan.

¹⁰Fear none of those things which thou shalt suffer: behold, the devil shall cast some of you into prison, that ye may be tried; and ye shall have tribulation ten days: be thou faithful unto death, and I will give thee a crown of life.

[11]He that hath an ear, let him hear what the Spirit saith unto the churches; He that overcometh shall not be hurt of the second death.

## 2. The Church at Philadelphia

**Revelation 3: 7–13:** [7]And to the angel of the church in Philadelphia write; These things saith he that is holy, he that is true, he that hath the key of David, he that openeth, and no man shutteth; and shutteth, and no man openeth;

[8]I know thy works: behold, I have set before thee an open door, and no man can shut it: for thou hast a little strength, and hast kept my word, and hast not denied my name.

[9]Behold, I will make them of the synagogue of Satan, which say they are Jews, and are not, but do lie; behold, I will make them to come and worship before thy feet, and to know that I have loved thee.

[10]Because thou hast kept the word of my patience, I also will keep thee from the hour of temptation, which shall come upon all the world, to try them that dwell upon the earth.

[11]Behold, I come quickly: hold that fast which thou hast, that no man takes thy crown.

[12]Him that overcometh will I make a pillar in the temple of my God, and he shall go no more out: and I will write upon him the name of my God, and the name of the city of my God, which is new Jerusalem, which cometh down out of heaven from my God: and I will write upon him my new name.

[13]He that hath an ear let him hear what the Spirit saith unto the churches.

## Things Church leaders carelessly do today:

- Some go to single sister's homes to pray for them alone. This to me is not right. It is a trap you may fall into. My advice is that you should take your wife along or ask a brother to follow you there.

In our church, most of the women's issues are taken care of by my wife and other women leaders, and it has been working just fine. I counsel women, but my secretary who is a brother must always be available too. In fact, he schedules most of my counseling appoint-ments.

The enemy is using women to tempt men of God today because of money. They would invite you to their homes as a pretense, and lure you into what you did not plan for. Even if someone is sick and your wife is not available to accompany you, let them call the emergency line instead of putting yourself into a bad and unexpected situation. Beware of where you go alone. Know when to say no, you are not God.

We must try as much as possible not to even counsel alone. Let your wife be involved or hand the case over to her. The fact though, is that most people we counsel are innocent; they do not plan evil, but lack the knowledge of the word of God. **We are to flee the appearance of evil.**

- We must not hire an office worker, especially a secretary, who will get us into trouble. This advice is not only for Spiritual leaders. This is also applicable to those Christians who run their own businesses. Beware of the naked dressed ladies, those who make you tea or coffee while wearing short skirts or skimpy tops that reveal their cleavages. A carelessly dressed worker is as dangerous as a serpent. When someone's dress is revealing all her body parts, we must do something about it as soon as possible. Many leaders, church or corporate, have gotten into trouble in the hands of seducers who called themselves Christians. Some have destroyed Pastor's families.

- Counseling women/men alone: In the past, men of God could counsel women, or men alone without any trouble. Today, things have changed because only God knows who is who in the kingdom. Just like in Jesus' days, those close to the leaders are the ones who get them into trouble, because they know their secrets and life history. They do this to make financial gains. They lie on you, sue you, and demand a big settlement. With liars, it is only a matter of time.

I heard a story about a Sister who lived with a Pastor. After God met her needs and she got married, she lied and said that the Pastor had an affair with her. Her parents who asked the Pastor to help her were against her claim. She later got thousands of dollars in settlement, only to have a stroke soon after and died.

People must fear God, who remains the same for ever more. He is a God of love and also a God of consuming fire. No one wants to experience His wrath.

If you are lying on a man or woman of God or a Christian for financial gain and it seems to be working for you, you need to repent and change because when God pulls the plug, you will regret the rest of your life if you refuse to repent.

# CHAPTER NINE

## THE HIDDEN TRAP OF FEAR

There are several things Pastors fear, and among them is **the fear of failure**. Leaders understand that you always fail more than you succeed, but they learn from their failures, and discover the more you try, the more successes you will achieve.

A second **fear is rejection**. Some Pastors are more concerned about what other Pastors think of them than they are their own congregation. Once Pastors form a structured "fellowship" there will always be a battle for leadership. Privileges and accolades will be granted or withheld by the Godfathers. Thus, the Pastor fears he might do something to offend those "who seemed to be somewhat" **(Galatians 2:6).**

**⁶ But of these who seemed to be somewhat, (what-soever they were, it maketh no matter to me: God accepteth no man's person :) for they who seemed to be somewhat in conference added nothing to me:**

The solution is to learn all you can about how to **"Pastor your church."** If all you are doing is preach-ing to the choir and reading books by those who are obsessed with "standards" they require of you; you will never overcome your fears. Confidence comes with learning, experience, and trust in the Lord.

**"The fear of the LORD is the beginning of wisdom: and the knowledge of the holy is understanding" (Proverbs 9:10).**

Leaders fear to train other or let others do what they do for fear of them taking over. One thing every traitor must know is that our calling is unique, and if you think you can run with another man's vision, you will crash. I made this statement in our church when the enemy came a few times in the past.

The solution is to seek God and let Him show you his will and purpose for your life and run with it.

Running with another man's destiny will get you into trouble. Traitors want something that is already cooked and ready. They do not want to start anything. A successful man either in the ministry or otherwise has stories to tell about how God brought him thus far. What traitors and Judas do not want to hear is the thus far.

The third Fear is **fear of Success**. Oh no, how can this be? You might question this phobia, and be the last to acknowledge its existence, but it is very real. Many pastors fear church growth. Success would mean more responsibility and commitment. Growth would mean change, and others would receive some of the attention enjoyed by the pastor. New babies demand a sharing of the toys.

Success means that someone else may be able to do things better than the Pastor, therefore many refuse to develop people or give important ministries to them. The Pastor becomes the bottleneck to growth. You cannot succeed unless you change, and success forces the church to change.

The final Fear – That is Common is **Giving Others** a Chance to do Most of the Things you do as a Pastor.

I strongly believe that the litmus test of a good leader is when the leader is not at home. Can the church function without you?

Will every department of the church still run smoothly without the Pastors around? Will the heads of departments still function if the Pastor travels? Can the company function without the manager? Can your family function without the dad? Will the engine oil be changed before daddy arrives home? Will the lawn be mowed if your husband is away for job assignment for three months?

One personal opinion which is also a fact is: if the Pastor is no more, the work of God will still go on. I understand that a Pastor, who is loved by the people, is expected to preach every Sunday. This is normal but not the best.

The few times in seven years that I travelled for two weeks, some of our members said they missed me when I came back. That does not mean others did not miss me. Some just cannot verbally express it. But thank God, some also said "But the minister who preached did a good job"

# A FEW REASONS PASTORS DO NOT GIVE OTHER PEOPLE A CHANCE

1. Some probably think others cannot handle the work well. This is mostly true because of the Pastor's anointing and experience, but it is not enough reason to do this.
2. Some probably think others do not have the vision, zeal, experience, or wisdom to do the work. This is also true in some cases, but giving others a chance could be an eye opener to the gifts and talents in people. Many gifts and talents are detected in the House of David mostly during different groups' conferences or programs. This is when members are given roles to minister, sing in the choir, be in the drama group or dance group, and even preach. We even allow Children to preach on a Sunday each year.

3. Some think the subordinates will outshine them if they are given a chance. One thing I do know is that we are unique individuals with unique talents and gifts. The Kingdom of God is not about competition. The way I preach is always going to be different from the way the rest of my ministers preach. The way I teach is different from the way all my ministers teach, so as a Pastor, I do not envy anyone at all. In fact as a spiritual father, I pray that my spiritual children should be better than me, not only in the things of God, but in all things. This is the reason why our church will have the best in every area of life. I encourage people to become all they can for God in their careers and also working in the House of David.

Jesus told his disciples in **the Holy Book in John 14:12, "Verily, verily, I say unto you, he that believeth on me, the works that I do shall he do also; and greater works than these shall he do; because I go unto my Father.**

A leader who will not give others under him a chance all because they will do better is not like Jesus. This is one of the reasons that the careers of ministers and workers are not growing.

**Exodus Chapters 18: 17 – 24:** [17]And Moses' father in law said unto him, the thing that thou doest is not good.

[18]Thou wilt surely wear away, both thou, and this people that is with thee: for this thing is too heavy for thee; thou art not able to perform it thyself alone.

[19]Hearken now unto my voice, I will give thee counsel, and God shall be with thee: Be thou for the people to God-ward, that thou mayest bring the causes unto God:

[20] And thou shalt teach them ordinances and laws, and shalt shew them the way wherein they must walk, and the work that they must do.

[21] Moreover thou shalt provide out of all the people able men, such as fear God, men of truth, hating covetousness; and place such over them, to be rulers of thousands, and rulers of hundreds, rulers of fifties, and rulers of tens:

[22] And let them judge the people at all seasons: and it shall be, that every great matter they shall bring unto thee, but every small matter they shall judge: so shall it be easier for thyself, and they shall bear the burden with thee.

[23] If thou shalt do this thing and God command thee so, then thou shalt be able to endure, and all this people shall also go to their place in peace.

[24] So Moses hearkened to the voice of his father in law, and did all that he had said.

**Exodus 31: 2 – 6** the Lord said to Moses "See, I have called by name Bezaleel...and I have filled him with the Spirit of God, in wisdom, and in under-standing, and in knowledge, and in all manner of workmanship, to devise cunning works, to work in gold, and in silver, and in brass, etc. And I behold, I have given with him Aholiab, the son of Ahisamach, of the tribe of Dan; and in the hearts of all that are wise-hearted I have put wisdom, that they may make all that I have commanded thee.

**Exodus chapters 36 to 40:** These men did a great job according to the command-ments that the Lord had given to Moses, yet Moses did not in any way diminish in the sight of the people nor in the sight of God – did everyone occupy his own place in the service and sight of God and the children of Israel.

**Exodus 36**

¹Then wrought Bezaleel and Aholiab, and every wise hearted man, in whom the LORD put wisdom and understanding to know how to work all manner of work for the service of the sanctuary, according to all that the LORD had commanded.

²And Moses called Bezaleel and Aholiab, and every wise hearted man, in whose heart the LORD had put wisdom, even every one whose heart stirred him up to come unto the work to do it:

³And they received of Moses all the offering, which the children of Israel had brought for the work of the service of the sanctuary, to make it withal. And they brought yet unto him free offerings every morning.

⁴And all the wise men, that wrought all the work of the sanctuary, came every man from his work which they made;

⁵And they spake unto Moses, saying, The people bring much more than enough for the service of the work, which the LORD commanded to make.

⁶And Moses gave commandment, and they caused it to be proclaimed throughout the camp, saying, let neither man nor woman make any more work for the offering of the sanctuary. So the people were restrained from bringing.

⁷For the stuff they had was sufficient for all the work to make it, and too much.

⁸And every wise hearted man among them that wrought the work of the tabernacle made ten curtains of fine twined linen, and blue, and purple, and scarlet: with cherubims of cunning work made he them.

⁹The length of one curtain was twenty and eight cubits, and the breadth of one curtain four cubits: the curtains were all of one size.

[10]And he coupled the five curtains one unto another: and the other five curtains he coupled one unto another.

[11]And he made loops of blue on the edge of one curtain from the selvedge in the coupling: likewise he made in the uttermost side of another curtain, in the coupling of the second.

[12]Fifty loops made he in one curtain, and fifty loops made he in the edge of the curtain which was in the coupling of the second: the loops held one curtain to another.

[13]And he made fifty taches of gold, and coupled the curtains one unto another with the taches: so it became one tabernacle.

[14]And he made curtains of goats' hair for the tent over the tabernacle: eleven curtains he made them.

[15]The length of one curtain was thirty cubits, and four cubits was the breadth of one curtain: the eleven curtains were of one size.

[16]And he coupled five curtains by themselves, and six curtains by themselves.

[17]And he made fifty loops upon the uttermost edge of the curtain in the coupling, and fifty loops made he upon the edge of the curtain which coupleth the second.

[18]And he made fifty taches of brass to couple the tent together, that it might be one.

[19]And he made a covering for the tent of rams' skins dyed red, and a covering of badgers' skins above that.

[20]And he made boards for the tabernacle of shittim wood, standing up.

<sup>21</sup>The length of a board was ten cubits, and the breadth of a board one cubit and a half.

<sup>22</sup>One board had two tenons, equally distant one from another: thus did he make for all the boards of the tabernacle.

<sup>23</sup>And he made boards for the tabernacle; twenty boards for the south side southward:

<sup>24</sup>And forty sockets of silver he made under the twenty boards; two sockets under one board for his two tenons, and two sockets under another board for his two tenons.

<sup>25</sup>And for the other side of the tabernacle, which is toward the north corner, he made twenty boards,

<sup>26</sup>And their forty sockets of silver; two sockets under one board, and two sockets under another board.

<sup>27</sup>And for the sides of the tabernacle westward he made six boards.

<sup>28</sup>And two boards made he for the corners of the tabernacle in the two sides.

<sup>29</sup>And they were coupled beneath, and coupled together at the head thereof, to one ring: thus he did to both of them in both the corners.

<sup>30</sup>And there were eight boards; and their sockets were sixteen sockets of silver, under every board two sockets.

<sup>31</sup>And he made bars of shittim wood; five for the boards of the one side of the tabernacle,

<sup>32</sup>And five bars for the boards of the other side of the tabernacle, and five bars for the boards of the tabernacle for the sides westward.

[33]And he made the middle bar to shoot through the boards from the one end to the other.

[34]And he overlaid the boards with gold, and made their rings of gold to be places for the bars, and overlaid the bars with gold.

[35]And he made a vail of blue, and purple, and scarlet, and fine twined linen: with cherubims made he it of cunning work.

[36]And he made thereunto four pillars of shittim wood, and overlaid them with gold: their hooks were of gold; and he cast for them four sockets of silver.

[37]And he made an hanging for the tabernacle door of blue, and purple, and scarlet, and fine twined linen, of needlework;

[38]And the five pillars of it with their hooks: and he overlaid their chapiters and their fillets with gold: but their five sockets were of brass.

## Exodus 37

[1]And Bezaleel made the ark of shittim wood: two cubits and a half was the length of it, and a cubit and a half the breadth of it, and a cubit and a half the height of it:

[2]And he overlaid it with pure gold within and without, and made a crown of gold to it round about.

[3]And he cast for it four rings of gold, to be set by the four corners of it; even two rings upon the one side of it, and two rings upon the other side of it.

[4]And he made staves of shittim wood, and overlaid them with gold.

⁵And he put the staves into the rings by the sides of the ark, to bear the ark.

⁶And he made the mercy seat of pure gold: two cubits and a half was the length thereof, and one cubit and a half the breadth thereof.

⁷And he made two cherubims of gold, beaten out of one piece made he them, on the two ends of the mercy seat;

⁸One cherub on the end on this side, and another cherub on the other end on that side: out of the mercy seat made he the cherubims on the two ends thereof.

⁹And the cherubims spread out their wings on high, and covered with their wings over the mercy seat, with their faces one to another; even to the mercy seatward were the faces of the cherubims.

¹⁰And he made the table of shittim wood: two cubits was the length thereof, and a cubit the breadth thereof, and a cubit and a half the height thereof:

¹¹And he overlaid it with pure gold, and made thereunto a crown of gold round about.

¹²Also he made thereunto a border of an handbreadth round about; and made a crown of gold for the border thereof round about.

¹³And he cast for it four rings of gold, and put the rings upon the four corners that were in the four feet thereof.

¹⁴Over against the border were the rings, the places for the staves to bear the table.

¹⁵And he made the staves of shittim wood, and overlaid them with gold, to bear the table.

[16]And he made the vessels which were upon the table, his dishes, and his spoons, and his bowls, and his covers to cover withal, of pure gold.

[17]And he made the candlestick of pure gold: of beaten work made he the candlestick; his shaft, and his branch, his bowls, his knops, and his flowers, were of the same:

[18]And six branches going out of the sides thereof; three branches of the candlestick out of the one side thereof, and three branches of the candlestick out of the other side thereof:

[19]Three bowls made after the fashion of almonds in one branch, a knop and a flower; and three bowls made like almonds in another branch, a knop and a flower: so throughout the six branches going out of the candlestick.

[20]And in the candlestick were four bowls made like almonds, his knops, and his flowers:

[21]And a knop under two branches of the same, and a knop under two branches of the same, and a knop under two branches of the same, according to the six branches going out of it.

[22]Their knops and their branches were of the same: all of it was one beaten work of pure gold.

[23]And he made his seven lamps, and his snuffers, and his snuff dishes, of pure gold.

[24]Of a talent of pure gold made he it, and all the vessels thereof.

[25]And he made the incense altar of shittim wood: the length of it was a cubit, and the breadth of it a cubit; it was foursquare; and two cubits was the height of it; the horns thereof were of the same.

²⁶And he overlaid it with pure gold, both the top of it, and the sides thereof round about, and the horns of it: also he made unto it a crown of gold round about.

²⁷And he made two rings of gold for it under the crown thereof, by the two corners of it, upon the two sides thereof, to be places for the staves to bear it withal.

²⁸And he made the staves of shittim wood, and over laid them with gold.

²⁹And he made the holy anointing oil, and the pure incense of sweet spices, according to the work of the apothecary.

## Exodus 38

¹And he made the altar of burnt offering of shittim wood: five cubits was the length thereof, and five cubits the breadth thereof; it was foursquare; and three cubits the height thereof.

²And he made the horns thereof on the four corners of it; the horns thereof were of the same: and he overlaid it with brass.

³And he made all the vessels of the altar, the pots, and the shovels, and the basons, and the fleshhooks, and the firepans: all the vessels thereof made he of brass.

⁴And he made for the altar a brasen grate of network under the compass thereof beneath unto the midst of it.

⁵And he cast four rings for the four ends of the grate of brass, to be places for the staves.

⁶And he made the staves of shittim wood, and overlaid them with brass.

[7]And he put the staves into the rings on the sides of the altar, to bear it withal; he made the altar hollow with boards.

[8]And he made the laver of brass, and the foot of it of brass, of the lookingglasses of the women assembling, which assembled at the door of the tabernacle of the congregation.

[9]And he made the court: on the south side southward the hangings of the court were of fine twined linen, an hundred cubits:

[10]Their pillars were twenty, and their brasen sockets twenty; the hooks of the pillars and their fillets were of silver.

[11]And for the north side the hangings were an hundred cubits, their pillars were twenty, and their sockets of brass twenty; the hooks of the pillars and their fillets of silver.

[12]And for the west side were hangings of fifty cubits, their pillars ten, and their sockets ten; the hooks of the pillars and their fillets of silver.

[13]And for the east side eastward fifty cubits.

[14]The hangings of the one side of the gate were fifteen cubits; their pillars three, and their sockets three.

[15]And for the other side of the court gate, on this hand and that hand, were hangings of fifteen cubits; their pillars three, and their sockets three.

[16]All the hangings of the court round about were of fine twined linen.

[17]And the sockets for the pillars were of brass; the hooks of the pillars and their fillets of silver; and the overlaying of their chapiters of silver; and all the pillars of the court were filleted with silver.

<sup></sup>¹⁸And the hanging for the gate of the court was needlework, of blue, and purple, and scarlet, and fine twined linen: and twenty cubits was the length, and the height in the breadth was five cubits, answerable to the hangings of the court.

¹⁹And their pillars were four, and their sockets of brass four; their hooks of silver, and the overlaying of their chapiters and their fillets of silver.

²⁰And all the pins of the tabernacle, and of the court round about, were of brass.

²¹This is the sum of the tabernacle, even of the tabernacle of testimony, as it was counted, according to the commandment of Moses, for the service of the Levites, by the hand of Ithamar, son to Aaron the priest.

²²And Bezaleel the son Uri, the son of Hur, of the tribe of Judah, made all that the LORD commanded Moses.

²³And with him was Aholiab, son of Ahisamach, of the tribe of Dan, an engraver, and a cunning workman, and an embroiderer in blue, and in purple, and in scarlet, and fine linen.

²⁴All the gold that was occupied for the work in all the work of the holy place, even the gold of the offering, was twenty and nine talents, and seven hundred and thirty shekels, after the shekel of the sanctuary.

²⁵And the silver of them that were numbered of the congregation was an hundred talents, and a thousand seven hundred and threescore and fifteen shekels, after the shekel of the sanctuary:

²⁶A bekah for every man, that is, half a shekel, after the shekel of the sanctuary, for every one that went to be numbered, from twenty years old and upward, for six hundred thousand and three thousand and five hundred and fifty men.

[27]And of the hundred talents of silver were cast the sockets of the sanctuary, and the sockets of the vail; an hundred sockets of the hundred talents, a talent for a socket.

[28]And of the thousand seven hundred seventy and five shekels he made hooks for the pillars, and overlaid their chapiters, and filleted them.

[29]And the brass of the offering was seventy talents, and two thousand and four hundred shekels.

[30]And therewith he made the sockets to the door of the tabernacle of the congregation, and the brasen altar, and the brasen grate for it, and all the vessels of the altar,

[31]And the sockets of the court round about, and the sockets of the court gate, and all the pins of the tabernacle, and all the pins of the court round about.

## Exodus 39

[1]And of the blue, and purple, and scarlet, they made cloths of service, to do service in the holy place, and made the holy garments for Aaron; as the LORD commanded Moses.

[2]And he made the ephod of gold, blue, and purple, and scarlet, and fine twined linen.

[3]And they did beat the gold into thin plates, and cut it into wires, to work it in the blue, and in the purple, and in the scarlet, and in the fine linen, with cunning work.

[4]They made shoulderpieces for it, to couple it together: by the two edges was it coupled together.

⁵And the curious girdle of his ephod, that was upon it, was of the same, according to the work thereof; of gold, blue, and purple, and scarlet, and fine twined linen; as the LORD commanded Moses.

⁶And they wrought onyx stones inclosed in ouches of gold, graven, as signets are graven, with the names of the children of Israel.

⁷And he put them on the shoulders of the ephod that they should be stones for a memorial to the children of Israel; as the LORD commanded Moses.

⁸And he made the breastplate of cunning work, like the work of the ephod; of gold, blue, and purple, and scarlet, and fine twined linen.

⁹It was foursquare; they made the breastplate double: a span was the length thereof, and a span the breadth thereof, being doubled.

¹⁰And they set in it four rows of stones: the first row was a sardius, a topaz, and a carbuncle: this was the first row.

¹¹And the second row, an emerald, a sapphire, and a diamond.

¹²And the third row, a ligure, an agate, and an amethyst.

¹³And the fourth row, a beryl, an onyx, and a jasper: they were inclosed in ouches of gold in their inclosing.

¹⁴And the stones were according to the names of the children of Israel, twelve, according to their names, like the engravings of a signet, everyone with his name, according to the twelve tribes.

¹⁵And they made upon the breastplate chains at the ends, of wreathen work of pure gold.

¹⁶And they made two ouches of gold, and two gold rings; and put the two rings in the two ends of the breastplate.

[17]And they put the two wreathen chains of gold in the two rings on the ends of the breastplate.

[18]And the two ends of the two wreathen chains they fastened in the two ouches, and put them on the shoulder pieces of the ephod, before it.

[19]And they made two rings of gold, and put them on the two ends of the breastplate, upon the border of it, which was on the side of the ephod inward.

[20]And they made two other golden rings, and put them on the two sides of the ephod underneath, toward the forepart of it, over against the other coupling thereof, above the curious girdle of the ephod.

[21]And they did bind the breastplate by his rings unto the rings of the ephod with a lace of blue, that it might be above the curious girdle of the ephod, and that the breastplate might not be loosed from the ephod; as the LORD commanded Moses.

[22]And he made the robe of the ephod of woven work, all of blue.

[23]And there was a hole in the midst of the robe, as the hole of a habergeon, with a band round about the hole that it should not rend.

[24]And they made upon the hems of the robe pomegranates of blue, and purple, and scarlet, and twined linen.

[25]And they made bells of pure gold, and put the bells between the pomegranates upon the hem of the robe, round about between the pomegranates;

[26]A bell and a pomegranate, a bell and a pomegranate, round about the hem of the robe to minister in; as the LORD commanded Moses.

<sup>27</sup>And they made coats of fine line of woven work for Aaron, and for his sons,

<sup>28</sup>And a mitre of fine linen, and goodly bonnets of fine linen, and linen breeches of fine twined linen,

<sup>29</sup>And a girdle of fine twined linen, and blue, and purple, and scarlet, of needlework; as the LORD commanded Moses.

<sup>30</sup>And they made the plate of the holy crown of pure gold, and wrote upon it writing, like to the engravings of a signet, HOLINESS TO THE LORD.

<sup>31</sup>And they tied unto it a lace of blue, to fasten it on high upon the mitre; as the LORD commanded Moses.

<sup>32</sup>Thus was all the work of the tabernacle of the tent of the congregation finished: and the children of Israel did according to all that the LORD commanded Moses, so did they.

<sup>33</sup>And they brought the tabernacle unto Moses, the tent, and all his furniture, his taches, his boards, his bars, and his pillars, and his sockets,

<sup>34</sup>And the covering of rams' skins dyed red, and the covering of badgers' skins, and the vail of the covering,

<sup>35</sup>The ark of the testimony, and the staves thereof, and the mercy seat,

<sup>36</sup>The table, and all the vessels thereof, and the shewbread,

<sup>37</sup>The pure candlestick, with the lamps thereof, even with the lamps to be set in order, and all the vessels thereof, and the oil for light,

<sup>38</sup>And the golden altar, and the anointing oil, and the sweet incense, and the hanging for the tabernacle door,

[39]The brasen altar, and his grate of brass, his staves, and all his vessels, the laver and his foot,

[40]The hangings of the court, his pillars, and his sockets, and the hanging for the court gate, his cords, and his pins, and all the vessels of the service of the tabernacle, for the tent of the congregation,

[41]The cloths of service to do service in the holy place, and the holy garments for Aaron the priest, and his sons' garments, to minister in the priest's office.

[42]According to all that the LORD commanded Moses, so the children of Israel made all the work.

[43]And Moses did look upon all the work, and, behold, they had done it as the LORD had commanded, and even so had they done it: and Moses blessed them.

**Exodus 40**

[1]And the LORD spake unto Moses, saying,

[2]On the first day of the first month shalt thou set up the tabernacle of the tent of the congregation.

[3]And thou shalt put therein the ark of the testimony, and cover the ark with the vail.

[4]And thou shalt bring in the table, and set in order the things that are to be set in order upon it; and thou shalt bring in the candlestick, and light the lamps thereof.

[5]And thou shalt set the altar of gold for the incense before the ark of the testimony, and put the hanging of the door to the tabernacle.

⁶And thou shalt set the altar of the burnt offering before the door of the tabernacle of the tent of the congregation.

⁷And thou shalt set the laver between the tent of the congregation and the altar, and shalt put water therein.

⁸And thou shalt set up the court round about, and hang up the hanging at the court gate.

⁹And thou shalt take the anointing oil, and anoint the tabernacle, and all that is therein, and shalt hallow it, and all the vessels thereof: and it shall be holy.

¹⁰And thou shalt anoint the altar of the burnt offering, and all his vessels, and sanctify the altar: and it shall be an altar most holy.

¹¹And thou shalt anoint the laver and his foot, and sanctify it.

¹²And thou shalt bring Aaron and his sons unto the door of the tabernacle of the congregation, and wash them with water.

¹³And thou shalt put upon Aaron the holy garments, and anoint him, and sanctify him; that he may minister unto me in the priest's office.

¹⁴And thou shalt bring his sons, and clothe them with coats:

¹⁵And thou shalt anoint them, as thou didst anoint their father that they may minister unto me in the priest's office: for their anointing shall surely be an everlasting priesthood throughout their generations.

¹⁶Thus did Moses: according to all that the LORD commanded him, so did he.

¹⁷And it came to pass in the first month in the second year, on the first day of the month, that the tabernacle was reared up.

[18]And Moses reared up the tabernacle, and fastened his sockets, and set up the boards thereof, and put in the bars thereof, and reared up his pillars.

[19]And he spread abroad the tent over the tabernacle, and put the covering of the tent above upon it; as the LORD commanded Moses.

[20]And he took and put the testimony into the ark, and set the staves on the ark, and put the mercy seat above upon the ark:

[21]And he brought the ark into the tabernacle, and set up the vail of the covering, and covered the ark of the testimony; as the LORD commanded Moses.

[22]And he put the table in the tent of the congregation, upon the side of the tabernacle northward, without the vail.

[23]And he set the bread in order upon it before the LORD; as the LORD had commanded Moses.

[24]And he put the candlestick in the tent of the congregation, over against the table, on the side of the tabernacle southward.

[25]And he lighted the lamps before the LORD; as the LORD commanded Moses.

[26]And he put the golden altar in the tent of the congregation before the vail:

[27]And he burnt sweet incense thereon; as the LORD commanded Moses.

[28]And he set up the hanging at the door of the tabernacle.

<sup>29</sup>And he put the altar of burnt offering by the door of the tabernacle of the tent of the congregation, and offered upon it the burnt offering and the meat offering; as the LORD commanded Moses.

<sup>30</sup>And he set the laver between the tent of the congregation and the altar, and put water there, to wash withal.

<sup>31</sup>And Moses and Aaron and his sons washed their hands and their feet thereat:

<sup>32</sup>When they went into the tent of the congregation, and when they came near unto the altar, they washed; as the LORD commanded Moses.

<sup>33</sup>And he reared up the court round about the tabernacle and the altar, and set up the hanging of the court gate. So Moses finished the work.

<sup>34</sup>Then a cloud covered the tent of the congregation, and the glory of the LORD filled the tabernacle.

<sup>35</sup>And Moses was not able to enter into the tent of the congregation, because the cloud abode thereon, and the glory of the LORD filled the tabernacle.

<sup>36</sup>And when the cloud was taken up from over the tabernacle, the children of Israel went onward in all their journeys:

<sup>37</sup>But if the cloud were not taken up, then they journeyed not till the day that it was taken up.

<sup>38</sup>For the cloud of the LORD was upon the tabernacle by day, and fire was on it by night, in the sight of all the house of Israel, throughout all their journeys.

A good leader raises others in order to take over after them. May we be like Jesus, Moses, Elijah, Paul, Peter and so on in Jesus name.

4. Finally, we cannot blame leaders who are court-eous about the above points. The reason is that some so called subordinates and assistants grow wings at some point. They start out with so much humility and genuine love of the cause. They follow diligently, dedicatedly, and serve God with all their hearts, souls and minds. Suddenly, envy gets into them and the devil now suggests they should plan and execute a takeover. Lie to your leaders, and you will become the Pastor in a jiffy. How many people know that anyone who is against you as a Christian is fighting against God? They cannot prevail even when they try.

Most of these kinds of people want to eat where they have not sowed. They are diligent, and dedicated because of what they want to carry out tomorrow, not because they love God or his vision. Nobody really knows what the Pastor's job entails.

They think it is all about Sunday Sermon and you go home. No wonder, the deflectors comes back to say to their Pastors "I didn't know what I got involved in"

These kinds of people never last. They end up regretting the rest of their lives. Their master – the devil was defeated and they shall be defeated at last.

Every Pastor or church leaders MUST yearly check your church registration with your state. Some of this follower's first step is to place their names on the church registration, and then attack. With their position in the church, they thought they could do anything which is against the law. If you have done this, repent.

If you are a victim of this, be encouraged. The Man of war Himself will fight His battle. He has never failed.

# CHAPTER TEN

## HIDDEN TRAP OF PRAISE OF MEN WITH HIDDEN AGENDA

We are going to use the story of Saul and David as a case study in this chapter.

## SAUL IN LOVE WITH DAVID

**1 Samuel 16:14-23:** [14] But the Spirit of the LORD departed from Saul, and an evil spirit from the LORD troubled him.

[15] And Saul's servants said unto him, Behold now, an evil spirit from God troubleth thee.

[16] Let our lord now command thy servants, which are before thee, to seek out a man, who is a cunning player on an harp: and it shall come to pass, when the evil spirit from God is upon thee, that he shall play with his hand, and thou shalt be well.

[17] And Saul said unto his servants, provide me now a man that can play well, and bring him to me.

[18] Then answered one of the servants, and said, Behold, I have seen a son of Jesse the Bethlehemite, that is cunning in playing, and a

mighty valiant man, and a man of war, and prudent in matters, and a comely person, and the LORD is with him.

[19] Wherefore Saul sent messengers unto Jesse, and said, send me David thy son, which is with the sheep.

[20] And Jesse took an ass laden with bread, and a bottle of wine, and a kid, and sent them by David his son unto Saul.

[21] And David came to Saul, and stood before him: and he loved him greatly; and he became his armour-bearer.

[22] And Saul sent to Jesse, saying, Let David, I pray thee, stand before me; for he hath found favour in my sight.

[23] And it came to pass, when the evil spirit from God was upon Saul, that David took a harp, and played with his hand: so Saul was refreshed, and was well, and the evil spirit departed from him.

# THE CHALLENGE OF GOLIATH

**1 Samuel 17:1-22:** [1] Now the Philistines gathered together their armies to battle, and were gathered together at Shochoh, which belongeth to Judah, and pitched between Shochoh and Azekah, in Ephes-dammim.

[2] And Saul and the men of Israel were gathered together, and pitched by the valley of Elah, and set the battle in array against the Philistines.

[3] And the Philistines stood on a mountain on the one side, and Israel stood on a mountain on the other side: and there was a valley between them.

[4] And there went out a champion out of the camp of the Philistines, named Goliath, of Gath, whose height was six cubits and a span.

[5] And he had an helmet of brass upon his head, and he was armed with a coat of mail; and the weight of the coat was five thousand shekels of brass.

[6] And he had greaves of brass upon his legs, and a target of brass between his shoulders.

[7] And the staff of his spear was like a weaver's beam; and his spear's head weighed six hundred shekels of iron: and one bearing a shield went before him.

[8] And he stood and cried unto the armies of Israel, and said unto them, Why are ye come out to set your battle in array? am not I a Philistine, and ye servants to Saul? Choose you a man for you, and let him come down to me.

[9] If he be able to fight with me, and to kill me, then will we be your servants: but if I prevail against him, and kill him, then shall ye be our servants, and serve us.

[10] And the Philistine said, I defy the armies of Israel this day; give me a man, that we may fight together.

[11] When Saul and all Israel heard those words of the Philistine, they were dismayed, and greatly afraid.

[12] Now David was the son of that Ephrathite of Bethlehemjudah, whose name was Jesse; and he had eight sons: and the man went among men for an old man in the days of Saul.

[13] And the three eldest sons of Jesse went and followed Saul to the battle: and the names of his three sons that went to the battle were Eliab the firstborn, and next unto him Abinadab, and the third Shammah.

[14] And David was the youngest: and the three eldest followed Saul.

[15] But David went and returned from Saul to feed his father's sheep at Bethlehem.

[16] And the Philistine drew near morning and evening, and presented himself forty days.

[17] And Jesse said unto David his son, Take now for thy brethren an ephah of this parched corn, and these ten loaves, and run to the camp of thy brethren;

[18] And carry these ten cheeses unto the captain of their thousand, and look how thy brethren fare, and take their pledge.

[19] Now Saul, and they, and all the men of Israel, were in the valley of Elah, fighting with the Philistines.

[20] And David rose up early in the morning, and left the sheep with a keeper, and took, and went, as Jesse had commanded him; and he came to the trench, as the host was going forth to the fight, and shouted for the battle.

[21] For Israel and the Philistines had put the battle in array, army against army.

[22] And David left his carriage in the hand of the keeper of the carriage, and ran into the army, and came and saluted his brethren.

# DAVID HEAR GOLIATH'S CHALLENGE

**1 Samuel 17:23-31:** [23] And as he talked with them, behold, there came up the champion, the Philistine of Gath, Goliath by name, out of the armies of the Philistines, and spake according to the same words: and David heard them.

²⁴ And all the men of Israel, when they saw the man, fled from him, and were sore afraid.

²⁵ And the men of Israel said, have ye seen this man that is come up? Surely to defy Israel is he come up: and it shall be, that the man who killeth him, the king will enrich him with great riches, and will give him his daughter, and make his father's house free in Israel.

²⁶ And David spake to the men that stood by him, saying, what shall be done to the man that killeth this Philistine, and taketh away the reproach from Israel? for who is this uncircumcised Philistine, that he should defy the armies of the living God?

²⁷ And the people answered him after this manner, saying, So shall it be done to the man that killeth him.

²⁸ And Eliab his eldest brother heard when he spake unto the men; and Eliab's anger was kindled against David, and he said, Why camest thou down hither? and with whom hast thou left those few sheep in the wilderness? I know thy pride, and the naughtiness of thine heart; for thou art come down that thou mightest see the battle.

²⁹ And David said, what have I now done? **Is there not a cause?**

³⁰ And he turned from him toward another and spake after the same manner: and the people answered him again after the former manner.

³¹ And when the words were heard which David spake, they rehearsed them before Saul: and he sent for him.

## DAVID KILLS GOLIATH WHEN SAUL COULD NOT DEFEAT HIM

**1 Samuel 17:32-58:** ³² And David said to Saul, Let no man's heart fail because of him; thy servant will go and fight with this Philistine.

[33] And Saul said to David, Thou art not able to go against this Philistine to fight with him: for thou art but a youth, and he a man of war from his youth.

[34] And David said unto Saul, Thy servant kept his father's sheep, and there came a lion, and a bear, and took a lamb out of the flock:

[35] And I went out after him, and smote him, and delivered it out of his mouth: and when he arose against me, I caught him by his beard, and smote him, and slew him.

[36] Thy servant slew both the lion and the bear: and this uncircumcised Philistine shall be as one of them, seeing he hath defied the armies of the living God.

[37] David said moreover, The LORD that delivered me out of the paw of the lion, and out of the paw of the bear, he will deliver me out of the hand of this Philistine. And Saul said unto David, Go, and the LORD be with thee.

[38] And Saul armed David with his armour, and he put an helmet of brass upon his head; also he armed him with a coat of mail.

[39] And David girded his sword upon his armour, and he assayed to go; for he had not proved it. And David said unto Saul, I cannot go with these; for I have not proved them. And David put them off him.

[40] And he took his staff in his hand, and chose him five smooth stones out of the brook, and put them in a shepherd's bag which he had, even in a scrip; and his sling was in his hand: and he drew near to the Philistine.

[41] And the Philistine came on and drew near unto David; and the man that bare the shield went before him.

⁴² And when the Philistine looked about, and saw David, he disdained him: for he was but a youth, and ruddy, and of a fair countenance.

⁴³ And the Philistine said unto David, Am I a dog that thou comest to me with staves? And the Philistine cursed David by his gods.

⁴⁴ And the Philistine said to David, Come to me, and I will give thy flesh unto the fowls of the air, and to the beasts of the field.

⁴⁵ Then said David to the Philistine, Thou comest to me with a sword, and with a spear, and with a shield: but I come to thee in the name of the LORD of hosts, the God of the armies of Israel, whom thou hast defied.

⁴⁶ This day will the LORD deliver thee into mine hand; and I will smite thee, and take thine head from thee; and I will give the carcases of the host of the Philistines this day unto the fowls of the air, and to the wild beasts of the earth; that all the earth may know that there is a God in Israel.

⁴⁷ And all this assembly shall know that the LORD saveth not with sword and spear: for the battle is the LORD's and he will give you into our hands.

⁴⁸ And it came to pass, when the Philistine arose, and came, and drew nigh to meet David that David hastened, and ran toward the army to meet the Philistine.

⁴⁹ And David put his hand in his bag, and took thence a stone, and slang it, and smote the Philistine in his forehead that the stone sunk into his forehead; and he fell upon his face to the earth.

⁵⁰ So David prevailed over the Philistine with a sling and with a stone, and smote the Philistine, and slew him; but there was no sword in the hand of David.

[51] Therefore David ran, and stood upon the Philistine, and took his sword, and drew it out of the sheath thereof, and slew him, and cut off his head therewith. And when the Philistines saw their champion was dead, they fled.

[52] And the men of Israel and of Judah arose, and shouted, and pursued the Philistines, until thou come to the valley, and to the gates of Ekron. And the wounded of the Philistines fell down by the way to Shaaraim, even unto Gath, and unto Ekron.

[53] And the children of Israel returned from chasing after the Philistines, and they spoiled their tents.

[54] And David took the head of the Philistine, and brought it to Jerusalem; but he put his armour in his tent.

[55] And when Saul saw David go forth against the Philistine, he said unto Abner, the captain of the host, Abner, whose son is this youth? And Abner said, as thy soul liveth, O king, I cannot tell.

[56] And the king said, Enquire thou whose son the stripling is.

[57] And as David returned from the slaughter of the Philistine, Abner took him, and brought him before Saul with the head of the Philistine in his hand.

[58] And Saul said to him, whose son art thou, thou young man? And David answered, I am the son of thy servant Jesse the Bethlehemite.

## SAUL BECAME JEALOUS OF DAVID AFTER WOMENS SANG

**1 Samuel 18:5-16:** [5] And David went out whither-soever Saul sent him, and behaved himself wisely: and Saul set him over the men of war, and he was accepted in the sight of all the people, and also in the sight of Saul's servants.

[6] And it came to pass as they came, when David was returned from the slaughter of the Philistine, that the women came out of all cities of Israel, singing and dancing, to meet King Saul, with tabrets, with joy, and with instruments of musick.

[7] And the women answered one another as they played, and said, Saul hath slain his thousands, and David his ten thousands.

[8] And Saul was very wroth, and the saying displeased him; and he said, they have ascribed unto David ten thousands, and to me they have ascribed but thousands: and what can he have more but the kingdom?

[9] And Saul eyed David from that day and forward.

[10] And it came to pass on the morrow, that the evil spirit from God came upon Saul, and he prophesied in the midst of the house: and David played with his hand, as at other times: and there was a javelin in Saul's hand.

[11] And Saul cast the javelin; for he said, I will smite David even to the wall with it. And David avoided out of his presence twice.

[12] And Saul was afraid of David, because the LORD was with him, and was departed from Saul.

[13] Therefore Saul removed him from him, and made him his captain over a thousand; and he went out and came in before the people.

[14] And David behaved himself wisely in all his ways; and the LORD was with him.

[15] Wherefore when Saul saw that he behaved himself very wisely, he was afraid of him.

[16] But all Israel and Judah loved David, because he went out and came in before them.

## THE SCRIPTURES ABOVE SUMMARIZE

- How David was loved by Saul who invited him to play Harp for him. Each time he plays, Saul was refreshed and was well and the evil spirit would depart from him.
- How Saul loved him dearly and made him to be his Armored Bearer.
- How Goliath challenged Saul and how David killed Goliath.
- How Saul became Jealous of David all because of one problem: The women were singing and dancing to meet King Saul, with trumpets, with joy, and with instruments of Music. The problem is not in their singing, but trouble started when they said that Saul hath slain his thousands and David his ten thousands. Saul became jealous of David and was looking for a way to kill him.

**Proverbs 29:5,** "A man that flattereth his neighbor spreadeth a net for his feet."

Pastors, leaders, heads of departments, heads of the families (Dads and Moms), departmental managers, business owners, beware of those who praise you when your ministry is going good, when they are praising you that you are the best in your department, in your family.

Appreciating someone is not the issue. There is nothing wrong in encouraging someone when they do a good job. The problem is when they have a hidden agenda and envy in their hearts. This is one of many traps in being a leaders or being a good worker either in the kingdom of God or in the secular world.

## SOLUTION TO PREVENT US FROM GETTING TRAPPED

### 1. Hide or store the Word of God in your heart

**Psalm 119:11, "I have stored up your Word in my heart that I might not sin against you."**

To store up is to treasure up. What are the treasures of your heart? We all have them, and it is foolish for us to think we don't. It is much healthier for us to take note of our treasures, and then for us to consider which of our heart's treasures tend to draw most of our affection.

How often is God's word at the top of your treasure list?

When we have treasured God's Word, it protects us from sin. What a wonderful truth! Why not make sure the Word of God is a to treasure in your life? Maybe take a three or four hour span and read your Bible?

### 2. Seek God with your whole heart

**Psalm 119:10, "With my whole heart I seek you; let me not wander from your commandments.!**

As the old hymn, "Come, Thou Fount of Every Blessing," by Robert Robinson says: *Let Thy goodness, like a fetter, Bind my wandering heart to Thee. Prone to wander, Lord, I feel it, Prone to leave the God I love;*

Have you ever noticed that your heart is prone to wander? Do you want God with all your heart right now? Or, is there something else that you want right now, and it is preventing you from desiring God and his Word? What are you pursuing right now? Is the cry of your heart, "let me not wander from your commandments!"?

## 3. Keep your way pure

**Psalm 119:9, "How can a young man keep his way pure? By guarding it according to your word."**

The Word of God is a wonderful way to keep our lives pure. It is a guard to us and a preventer of evil. It provides a strength that can be found nowhere else.

How does the Word of God fit into your life? Are there other things that have more importance?

## 4. Keep a close watch yourself and on the teaching.

**1 Timothy 4:16, "Keep a close watch on yourself and on the teaching. Persist in this, for by so doing you will save both yourself and your hearers."**

Without realizing it, we can become careless. We can forget to pay close attention to myself, and our sin-loving flesh begins to weave its way into our daily life. But not only into my behavior, but also into my teaching! Godly behavior and godly teaching are inseparable. This is seen over and over again throughout the Scriptures, and yet, it is hard for us to keep in mind.

## 5. Trusting in God

Proverbs 3: 5-6, "Trust in the LORD with all thine heart; and lean not unto thine own understanding. ⁶In all thy ways acknowledge him and he shall direct thy paths.

# DECISION PAGE SPECIAL INVITATION

If you the reader of this book is not saved, I will like to remind you that salvation is FREE for the asking. Take a moment wherever you may be and ask the Lord to forgive you of your sins. Begin to repent of your sins, ask the Lord Jesus to come into your heart and take over your life.

If you have spoken these few simple words in truth, you are saved, and now you have eternal life. Also if you are saved but you know from your heart that you are not a serious Christian, please take a moment to rededicate your life to Christ and stay committed to God. **(I John 1:8-10, John 3:16).**

Please contact us at the number below for, prayer ministration, counseling, and questions.

Contact Address: Pastor Tai Olamigoke
6603 Langham Dr. NW, Houston, Texas 77084
Phone: 713-264-1650; 281-855-9540
Email: tolamigoke@hotmail.com

# THE AUTHOR AT A GLANCE

Pastor Tai, knew the Lord at a tender age of 13, is a man with passion both for God and things of God.

In his early days in the United States, Tai became Microsoft Certified Systems Engineer after working for few years in Nigeria as a Mechanical Engineer, and has worked with a number of IT firms as a Systems Analyst, Network Engineer/Administrator, System and Lead Field Engineer.

Pastor Tai also received a BA in Biblical Studies from Caroline University of Theology, MA degree in Christian Counseling Psychology and Doctorate of Ministry in Counseling from The Redeemer Bible College and Seminar.

Pastor Tai loves souls and spends most of his time reaching the unreachable and touching the untouch-able and feeding the hungry. While in India as a student, he joined the University fellowship and preached the Word mostly in villages. He and his friends were attacked several times, but God was with them.

Pastor Tai was called into the ministry in 1983 after God miraculously healed him of an incurable disease that almost took his life in his early age. He obeyed God and started teaching Bible study in two secondary schools. He joined Deeper Life Bible Church where he taught the Word of God and interpreted the Bible for his Pastor.

Pastor Tai was ordained by Apostle (Dr). Jerlet Mickie of New Light Church of God in Virginia. While at New Light, he was the Outreach Pastor. He fed the poor, distributed food to the needy and clothed them. During his last feeding, his group fed about 300 homeless people in Washington DC before his relocation to Houston Texas in 2001. He went on a three weeks mission to Okinawa Japan with his Pastor in 1999 where he helped the local churches in various ways. He ministered to Okinawa University students on this trip. Since his family moved to Houston, he has been on mission trips to Kuwait, Belize, Nicaragua and Canada.

Relocating to Houston Texas in 2001, Pastor Tai and his family prayerfully choose to join The Redeemed Christian Church of God where he was ordained a Pastor by Daddy Pastor E.A. Adeboye, the general overseer of the RCCG-world-wide.

In 2004, the Lord who called him earlier led Pastor Tai to start a Parish called House of David with about five families. House of David parish was inaugurated on November 14, 2004 and became one of the over seven thousand (7000) parishes of the The Redeemed Christian Church of God (worldwide).

Today, Pastor Tai and his members feed the community, clothe and care for them. Also by the grace of God, House of David added Church services in Spanish almost ten (10) years ago.

Pastor Tai and his wife, Caroline is happily married and has two wonderful children who are great examples and whom they are very proud of and blessing to our generation. No doubt we attribute all the glory and honor to God for everything and for all He has done for us all!

Printed in the United States
by Baker & Taylor Publisher Services